Drownproofing Techniques

D1519468

Drownproofing Techniques

for Floating, Swimming, and Open-water Survival

Reagh C. Wetmore, Ed. D.
Director of Aquatics and
Head Coach Men and Women's Swimming
Boston University
Boston, Massachusetts

THE STEPHEN GREENE PRESS
BRATTLEBORO, VERMONT

Copyright © 1981 by THE STEPHEN GREENE PRESS

Produced in the UNITED STATES OF AMERICA.
Designed by ROBERT R. ANDERSON and DOUGLAS KUBACH.
Page layout by IRVING PERKINS ASSOCIATES.
Published by THE STEPHEN GREENE PRESS, Fessenden Road, Brattleboro, Vermont 05301.

Library of Congress Cataloging in Publication Data

Wetmore, Reagh C. 1923–
    Drownproofing techniques for floating, swimming, and open-water survival.

    Bibliography: p. 163
    Includes index.
    1. Swimming.   2. Drowning—Prevention.   I. Title.
GV837.W47   797.2'1'0289   81-42
ISBN 0-8289-0410-3 (pbk.)

To Leslie, my wife, whose patience and understanding were invaluable, who typed the manuscript, and who—as a nonswimmer— through the use of drownproofing techniques, learned to swim during the preparation of this book.

Contents

Acknowledgments

To William Wasserman, whose photographs appear on the following pages. And to John Allen, Gary Geissler, Pat Leahy, Tom McGuinness and Terri Sullivan, who appear in the photographs.

Drownproofing Techniques

Introduction
Drownproofing Dimensions and Priorities

One day, two men in their early sixties were fishing off Cape Cod when they suddenly fell from their motorboat, which sped away from them. They found themselves about two miles from shore in a rough sea without life jackets. After floating around for a while, they made the decision to swim to shore. They used the drownproofing techniques, and when they reached the beach a few hours later, they found that they were not exhausted and felt they could have gone farther. Neither man was an expert swimmer in top condition, and both admitted they might not have survived had the incident happened before they learned drownproofing.

Many years ago, a flight to the West Indies crashed in the Caribbean sea. Before the wrecked plane sank, one woman managed to crawl out and into the water. She wore no life jacket and had no floating wreckage to cling to. After twenty hours of drownproof floating she was still alive when rescuers spotted her.

In special tests, hundreds of college and high school students floated and swam four to eight hours with their wrists tied behind their backs using drownproofing techniques. They stopped because of boredom, not distress.

Another woman, in her early thirties, remained a non-swimmer after several attempts at learning the crawl stroke. Her husband would not let her go canoeing with him and their children unless she learned how to swim. She had tried to learn previously many times, but could not swim more than a few strokes. She worked diligently at drownproofing and after ten, 1-hour sessions, completed two miles around the pool using the drownproof travel stroke. Her husband could not believe her accomplishment, but when invited to the pool to watch his wife he commented, "She looks so comfortable in the water you would think she had been swimming most of her life! I expected much less."

There have been thousands of nonswimming adults who have learned the drownproofing techniques to the extent that they could swim more than one mile and float at least one hour. Thousands of other adults who can swim have learned drownproofing techniques because of their survival value. For those who can't swim, drownproofing has provided a means of learning to swim and float before learning other strokes. Many adults never do learn the crawl stroke to a degree of efficiency. Others cannot swim the breast stroke because of the intricate leg action involved. Most can swim the elementary backstroke, but don't like it because they can't see where they are going and find the backstroke uncomfortable in rough water when waves wash over their faces.

The travel stroke may be used for people who want to learn to swim in an easy manner, and to be able to swim a long distance with little effort. In addition, drownproof floating provides an excellent way for resting in deep water. The built-in life jacket that people always have available— namely, their lungs when filled with air—helps keep the body afloat.

At one drownproofing clinic conducted by the author, several swimming instructors, having received training in drownproofing, were asked to teach the techniques to a number of nonswimmers six to fourteen years of age. These children had just completed six swimming lessons under the guidance of another instructor, but had not yet learned to swim. Each instructor in the clinic was asked to teach one child. In two hours all the children were floating and swimming in deep water using drownproofing techniques, and some were able to swim a few laps around the pool. Their original instructor came running down to the pool deck yelling: "You should not have those children in deep water—they can't swim!" A reply was quickly made, "They can now!"

The incidents cited above are typical of numerous demonstrations which have consistently supported the premise that drownproofing techniques and the Drownproofing Method make people safe in the water in a relatively short period of time.

As I watched increasing numbers of children who were nonswimmers learn drownproofing techniques before other aquatic skills, I became convinced that instruction in drownproofing techniques (i.e. floating and travel stroke) should take precedence over other aquatic skills in the initial stages of learning to swim. Many times children learn the crawl stroke first and are left with a swimming skill that allows them to plow through the water expending tremendous amounts of energy. Unfortunately, endurance or lack of endurance brings the swimming to a sudden halt when fatigue sets in. The distance most young children can swim the crawl stroke is usually between fifty and two hundred yards. The talented, who later become trained in competitive swimming, obviously can swim much further, but the child of low or average ability cannot swim far with the crawl stroke. However, children from four to seven are able to swim a mile using the travel stroke in eight to twelve sessions. I often wonder how many swimming instructors have started with a nonswimmer and have worked with the nonswimmer until that person was able to complete *a mile* swim. This accomplishment would be one of the excellent criteria for certification of instructors.

Swimming coaches and instructors have repeatedly said children get bored while they learn drownproof floating. Not one of these teachers and coaches was aware of the travel stroke. Admittedly, to teach drownproof floating to children exclusively would be a boring process for both instructor and learner, because the child stays in one position over an extended period of time. Lesson after lesson of this technique would become tedious and probably intolerable. Drownproofing instructors who know their business, therefore, teach drownproof floating and travel stroke simultaneously, spending a few minutes on each technique. First, youngsters learn how to stay afloat at or near the surface, coming up for air every five or six seconds. Then, with the same periodic breathing technique, they learn to move through the water using the long travel stroke. In a few sessions, most children find themselves covering a distance of one or two hundred yards—far more than their neighbors who, in the meantime, have learned the crawl stroke and may be able to complete a distance of sixty feet.

Drownproofing instructors have found that children who are nonswimmers, after receiving instructions in drownproof floating and drownproof swimming, are able to sustain themselves at or near the surface for substantially longer periods, and swim longer distances in much less time, than children who initially learn the crawl stroke.

The effortless way a skilled swimmer moves through the water provides a sharp contrast to the actions of the inexperienced beginner who is apt to flail frantically and struggle to get air. Swimmers who feel relaxed and secure in the water are able to enjoy the varied activities provided by a water environment. Although mastery of drownproofing techniques does not guarantee immunity from drowning, it does make it possible for almost anyone to survive in water for long periods with minimal fatigue. Tests have shown the unique adaptability of drownproofing techniques to long immersion, distance swimming, rough water, encumbrance of clothes, muscle cramps, and injury to limbs.

An understanding of the use of the body's buoyancy to conserve energy has helped many beginners and unskilled swimmers overcome their fear of deep water. Early instruction is designed to enable most people to swim a mile or more and to be able to sustain themselves at or near the surface for at least an hour.

Practically everyone can learn drownproofing. The floating and swimming strokes have been taught to many children with complete success. The elderly who can enter water, teenagers, college students, and other adults, when taught drownproofing techniques, are all able to catch on with equal ease. When certain physically disabled people who have the use of two or more limbs learn drownproofing, they are as safe in the water as anyone else. Security in the water is no longer limited to good swimmers but is attainable by almost everyone regardless of age, sex, or physical condition.

Drownproofing is a set of floating and swimming techniques which enables swimmers to use body buoyancy to conserve energy. These techniques are basic to safe swimming. Drownproofing trains people to float for long periods and swim long distances in rough water, even while fully clothed and afflicted with muscle cramps or injury to limbs.

Soon after drownproofing was developed by its originator, Fred Lanoue, the method gained recognition because of its use during World War II. Drownproofing techniques were used in teaching naval personnel how to survive if cast into water as a result of torpedo bombings. Many of these servicemen who were weak swimmers or nonswimmers found that use of drownproofing techniques enabled them to float around in deep water for long periods.

Following World War II, schools, yacht clubs, camps, and

colleges began to include drownproofing techniques in their programs. The American Red Cross, Y.M.C.A., and Boy Scouts soon adapted drownproof floating as a survival float. Later, the U.S. Marines began teaching drownproofing at their training base on Parris Island. More recently, continuing and outdoor education groups, community and recreation centers, colleges, schools, and camps, all in increasing numbers, have added drownproofing to their curricula.

More and more people in the field of aquatic activities are teaching drownproofing techniques. Drownproofing instructors believe it is of prime importance to learn at the outset those techniques which enable people to stay at the surface of deep water for extended periods of time with minimal fatigue, whatever the conditions. People become safe in the water when they learn to swim long distances and float long periods in rough water while fully clad, without suffering from fatigue. They are also safe when they can swim while afflicted with cramps or injury to limbs, and when they can cope with panic-provoking situations.

In recent years, editors and reporters of numerous magazines and newspapers have become impressed with the accomplishments of people who use drownproofing techniques. Producers of national network television and radio programs along with several local stations throughout the country have exposed the American public to drownproofing. Industrial executives, college presidents, school principals, directors of camps, coordinators of continuing and outdoor education groups, supervisors of community centers and recreation programs have written to inquire about the techniques or to express enthusiasm about drownproofing programs. This growing interest no doubt means that in the near future, instruction in drownproofing will be available to nearly everyone and will be taught as the first and most important set of aquatic skills to be learned. There appears to

Drownproofing

be a consensus that drownproofing should be a priority for everyone.

Several years ago, the author conducted a drownproofing program for over one hundred children. A list of these children who completed a one-mile swim was published in the local newspaper. Enrollment in the program soon doubled because parents realized their children were acquiring skills that provided maximum protection against swimming-related emergencies.

Parents who learn drownproofing are able to teach the techniques to their children. Anyone who carefully follows the instructions in this book, and who can perform the drownproofing techniques well enough to be able to swim one mile and float one hour ought to be able to teach others to do the same. The techniques are relatively simple and the progressive lessons offered on these pages have been followed successfully by thousands of instructors and learners.

1: Drownproofing
Techniques

TROUBLE IN THE WATER

Whenever a crisis confronts a swimmer or a nonswimmer—a fall into deep water, long immersion, a strong current pulling toward open sea—reason is often blotted out by fear. Inexperienced swimmers may try swimming against moving water while wearing heavy, waterlogged clothes; they may make ill-timed gasps for air while waves wash over their heads. They may exhaust themselves trying to keep their heads out of water, a particularly senseless step that is equivalent to supporting a ten- to twelve-pound brick above the surface. Muscle cramps, a common occurence, often frighten swimmers to even more frantic flailing, quickening exhaustion.

LIMITATIONS OF BASIC SWIMMING TECHNIQUES

Countless hours are spent teaching youngsters to tread water, swim on their backs, and do the crawl stroke. However, none of these techniques provides maximum security against water hazards. Treading water is effective for momentary orientation, but prolonged immersion with the head held above the water brings on fatigue.

Back swimming or back floating is restful in calm water, but presents the danger of choking when waves wash over the face. In addition, few swimmers have enough buoyancy to float motionless on their backs. Back floating is not a natural floating position. When completely relaxed, the majority of swimmers will return to a face-down floating position.

The crawl stroke became popular because it was designed for speed swimming. However, the alternate recovery of the arms above water limits the effectiveness of the crawl as a resting or survival stroke because buoyancy is reduced.

NATURAL FLOATING POSITION

A. Back floating is not a natural floating position.

Drownproofing

B. When completely relaxed, the body will rotate forward.

C. The body stabilizes when in a face-down floating position.

ADAPTATION TO A WATER ENVIRONMENT

Anyone who uses the drownproofing techniques minimizes exhaustion by taking advantage of the body's natural buoyancy to stay afloat and swim without supporting head or limbs above water. Panic is controlled since the method assures an ample supply of air despite high waves, cramps, or heavy clothes. Drownproof floating and swimming techniques have been adapted to accommodate all types of floaters as well as the nonbuoyant.

FLOATERS AND SINKERS

The average human, with lungs filled with air, floats with about 99 percent of the body beneath the surface—an important fact because it means that most people can float if they keep their bodies at the *natural floating level.* The ratio of bone and muscle to fat and air governs an individual's floatability. Fat and air help to keep one afloat whereas, bone and muscle contribute to negative buoyancy. Drownproof floating and swimming techniques are modified for each of three body-buoyancy types, as shown in the accompanying chart.

BODY BUOYANCY

The application of drownproof floating and swimming techniques is facilitated by an understanding of body buoyancy, breath control, and energy conservation. Drownproofing instructors constantly advise swimmers to use body buoyancy to reduce effort. Breath control is vital because buoyancy is affected by the amount of air held in the lungs.

Individuals differ in terms of the ratio of body volume to

body weight. Specific gravity (which compares weight of an object to weight of an equal volume of water) of the human body varies from 0.96 to 1.20. Specific gravity of water is 1.00. People who have a specific gravity of less than 1.00 displace a volume of water greater than their own weight and tend to float. Those individuals whose specific gravity is more than 1.00 displace a volume of water less than their own weight and tend to sink.

Body type and vital capacity are two factors which determine an individual's buoyancy. Each human contains different components of bone, muscle, and fat. The specific gravity of bone has beeen calculated to be 1.900, of muscle 1.080, and of fat between 0.700 and 0.800. Bone and muscle tissue sink, while fat tissue floats. Muscular people with large bones tend toward negative buoyancy. Fat individuals and slender, light-boned ones tend to float.

Drownproofing Techniques and
Body-Buoyancy Types

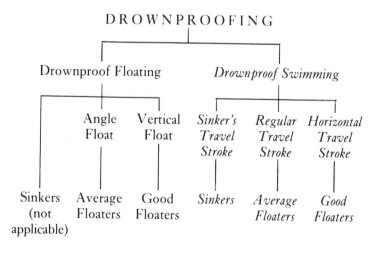

Vital capacity refers to the amount of air taken in by an individual in one inhalation. Body buoyancy increases when the lungs are filled with air because the volume of the body is increased without significantly altering the weight. Vital capacity varies considerably among different individuals. A reasonably accurate index to human buoyancy appears to be the relationship of vital capacity to body weight/volume ratio. This explains why maximum displacement by maximum submersion is of utmost importance when swimmers perform drownproofing techniques. The swimmers rest at their natural floating levels and let air and water do the work of support.

The progression for learning drownproofing techniques differs for each body-buoyancy type. In the chart opposite, items are marked which must be completed by sinkers, average floaters, and good floaters.

Buoyancy Test

A simple buoyancy test categorizes body-buoyancy type. A swimmer starts by placing himself side to the pool wall, or dock if at lake or ocean, and holds on to the gutter with one hand. The body is held in the vertical position. A deep breath is taken by inhaling for three or four seconds. The swimmer slowly leans forward with back curled until the trunk is about 45 degrees from vertical. The face is well in the water with the back of the neck and head at the surface. When the body is stable the swimmer carefully releases his hold on the gutter and arms and legs are allowed to dangle downward. The swimmer must hold his breath during the entire test, until a stable position of the legs is attained and noted.

An average floater is one who, with lungs filled with air, floats face down while the legs dangle in the water between vertical and 45 degrees from vertical. A good floater's body

LEARNING PROGRESSION
FOR EACH BODY-BUOYANCY TYPE

Body-Buoyancy Type	Buoyancy Test	DROWNPROOF FLOATING				DROWNPROOF SWIMMING		
		Breathing Drill	Breathing Stroke Drill	Angle Float	Vertical Float	Sinker's Travel Stroke	Regular Travel Stroke	Horizontal Travel Stroke
Sinkers	X	X				X[1]		
Average Floaters	X	X	X	X			X	
Good Floaters	X	X	X	X[2]	X			X

1. Sinkers who have high negative buoyancy may prefer the horizontal travel stroke.
2. Some good floaters may choose the angle float.

After a deep breath is inhaled while holding on to the gutter, face is put in water. After body is stable, hand is slowly removed from gutter. Swimmer holds breath five or six seconds until a stable position of legs can be observed.

and legs rise above 45 degrees or almost to a horizontal position. Even with lungs filled with air, nonbuoyant individuals cannot float without motion: a few remain suspended about one or two feet beneath the surface—others sink to bottom. The buoyancy test should be repeated three or four times to firmly establish body types.

BUOYANCY TEST: AVERAGE FLOATER

A. *Average floater: legs between vertical and 45 degrees above vertical.*

BUOYANCY TEST: GOOD FLOATER

B. *Good floater: legs 45 degrees or more above vertical.*

C. Sinker will not remain at surface while motionless.

All types of randomly selected people—including children, men and women of all ages—have been tested for buoyancy in the United States, and it has been found that approximately 54 percent are average floaters, 45 percent are good floaters, and 1 percent are nonbuoyant (sinkers). Thirty percent of athletes are nonbuoyant. Women are far more buoyant than men. About one of 100 males is nonbuoyant, whereas only one of 1,000 females is negatively buoyant. Both middle-aged men and women tend to be good floaters, whereas a high percentage of teenagers possess low positive buoyancy. Nearly all infants and young children are floaters.

2: Drownproof Floating

BREATHING AND BREATH CONTROL

Few people have enough buoyancy to float or swim for extended periods (while holding their heads above the surface) without expending excessive amounts of energy. Swimmers should learn how to hold their breaths underwater, to exhale underwater, and to be able repeatedly to get a proper exchange of air. While learning drownproofing techniques, conscious breath control becomes a crucial factor, because the buoyancy of a swimmer is greatly affected by the amount of air in the lungs.

BREATHING FLOAT DRILL FOR AVERAGE FLOATERS

Average floaters place themselves side to the pool and hold the gutter with one hand. After a deep breath is taken the head is submerged and the trunk angled forward. In five or six seconds the head is slowly tilted upward while the swimmer exhales through the nose. Exhalation is continued until the nose and mouth clear the surface. Inhalation does not begin until all the drops of water have been blown away from the nose and mouth. When inhalation is complete the head is tilted downward into the water.

*A. Body is side to wall while one hand grasps gutter. Free arm
and legs dangle loosely downward. Trunk is angled forward.
Swimmer stays in this position four to six seconds. Exhalation
begins as head is tilted upward and continues until nose and
mouth are above surface.*

B. *Inhalation begins after drops of water have been blown away from nose and mouth. Head is then tilted downward into water as body returns to angle-float position.*

BREATHING FLOAT DRILL
FOR GOOD FLOATERS

The swimmer begins by placing the entire front of the body against the pool wall, arms fully extended sidewards at level of shoulders, and thumbs looped over edge of the gutter. (Bottom of chin should be at water surface.) A deep breath is taken and the body is allowed to sink to its natural floating level. With the mouth and nostrils in the water a breath is held for about six seconds. The lips are kept tightly closed to keep water out of the mouth. A gentle downward press with the thumbs lifts the body slowly upward. Exhalation is done on the way up through the nose, and is continued until the nose and mouth are out of water. Air is then inhaled through the mouth. Air must be inhaled not swallowed.

BREATHING FLOAT DRILL
FOR GOOD FLOATERS

A. Swimmer stays in floating position four to six seconds. Body is raised by pressing down with thumbs. Air is exhaled during lift of body.

B. Press of thumbs and exhalation is continued until chin is level with surface. Air is then inhaled, after which body returns to original floating position.

To practice breathing some good floaters must overcome the body's tendency to float horizontally. Instead of placing the hands along the ledge of the pool they are placed under the rung of a ladder. This position will hold the body vertically.

VARIATION OF BREATHING DRILL FOR GOOD FLOATERS

Good floaters place palms under rung of ladder.

Swimmers who fear deep water can practice in shallow water by bending their legs. This drill allows beginners to experience the feeling of weightlessness in the water while learning to get a proper exchange of air.

BREATHING DRILL FOR BEGINNERS

Unskilled and nonswimmers can practice in shallow water by bending knees.

BREATHING STROKE DRILL FOR AVERAGE FLOATERS

The body is placed side to the wall while the swimmer grasps the gutter with one hand. The swimmer takes a deep breath, leans forward, and floats face down in an angled position. The free arm is lifted and crossed in front of the

BREATHING STROKE DRILL FOR AVERAGE FLOATERS

A. Swimmer floats face down four to six seconds with one hand on gutter.

Drownproofing

head. Exhalation begins as the head is tilted upward. When the nose and mouth emerge, a sideward and downward stroke is taken and the swimmer inhales. The swimmer then returns to the floating position.

B. When swimmer is ready to breathe the free arm is raised and crossed in front of head. Legs separate forward and backward.

C. *Head is tilted upward during exhalation. When head emerges, a sideward stroke is begun and swimmer inhales. Legs are brought together.*

D. *Arm circles backward behind shoulder and downward as swimmer returns to floating position.*

BREATHING STROKE DRILL
FOR GOOD FLOATERS

Good floaters combine a stroking movement with breathing by grasping the gutter with one hand and keeping the body in a vertical position side to the wall. After a deep breath is taken the swimmer sinks to the natural buoyancy level. The breath is held for five or six seconds. The free arm is then raised and

BREATHING STROKE DRILL
FOR GOOD FLOATERS

A. Swimmer starts in vertical position at natural floating level. One hand grasps the gutter. This position is held four to six seconds.

Drownproofing

crossed in front of the face as the legs separate. Exhalation is begun as the free arm strokes sideward. When the free arm has moved through a 90 degree angle, inhalation begins and continues until the arm circles backward behind the shoulder and downward. The legs are brought together and the swimmer returns to the vertical floating position.

B. Free arm is raised and crossed in front of face. Legs separate forward and backward.

BREATHING STROKE DRILL
FOR GOOD FLOATERS cont.

C. Exhalation begins as free arm begins to stroke sideward and legs move toward one another. Body begins to rise.

D. Inhalation begins as chin is level with surface. Arm stroke passes behind shoulder. Legs are brought together.

E. *Free arm circles backward and downward as body returns to natural floating level.*

DROWNPROOF FLOATING STROKE

The stroke used in both forms of drownproof floating (*angle* and *vertical*) creates sufficient lift force to sustain the head above the surface during inhalation with minimal effort. This lift force can be understood in terms of *Bernouilli's Principle:* "a change in speed of fluid flow over an object affects upward or downward pressure of the fluid on an object. If speed of flow is increased pressure is reduced, or if speed of flow is reduced pressure is increased." For example, speed of air flow over the bottom surface of an airplane wing, due to its shape and tilt, is slower than speed of air flow over the top surface of the wing. A higher pressure is developed under the wing than on the top surface which results in an upward push or lift.

When a tilted hand moves sideward through the water, the same type of pressure differential is created. The angle of the hands with the palms tilted outward produces a lower speed of water flow under the palms than on the top surface of the hands. A greater pressure under the hands is developed than on the upper surfaces, thereby creating a lift force. If the arms are moved slowly sideward, this lift force is sustained long enough to keep the head above the water while air is inhaled.

An excellent example of the lift force developed by a sideward stroke is demonstrated when a swimmer performs the drownproof vertical float. After air is inhaled, the body is allowed to float at the natural floating level with arms at sides. The water surface is usually somewhere between the eyebrows and hairline. The arms are raised and crossed in front of the shoulders. The arms then stroke sideward with palms tilted slightly outward, which causes the body to rise three to six inches—enough to allow a swimmer to get sufficient air to continue floating without motion for six to ten seconds.

Swimmers who use a sideward action of the arms for both

the angle and vertical float keep their shoulders at or near the surface. A downward thrust of the arms results in excessive bobbing, which tends to sink the body far below the surface.

ANGLE FLOAT

Drownproofing

ANGLE FLOAT

The angle float, designed for average floaters, is based on the knowledge that when relaxed, average floaters will float in a face-down vertical or semi-vertical position with the arms and legs dangling loosely downward. When the swimmer is ready to breathe, the arms are lifted in front of the body with the thumbs up. The head must remain still until the wrists are crossed near the surface. Then the head is tilted upward while the swimmer exhales slowly. As the chin emerges from the water a sideward stroke is started with the hands angled about 45 degrees palms outward. With the hands pitched at this angle a sufficient lift force is created to easily sustain the head above the surface while air is inhaled. The sideward and downward stroke must be performed while the head is out of the water to counteract sinking. When the head is lifted out of water the body should remain angled forward. If necessary, a scissor kick may be used to balance the body. The swimmer floats six to ten seconds between breaths in a natural floating position.

Floating Position

The most important part of the angle float is the floating position. Swimmers should feel completely relaxed while holding their breath. There should be no tension in the back of the neck (head is allowed to float), shoulders, lower back or hips (arms and legs must be limp). This position is sustained for six to ten seconds.

Breathing

If the breath is held for less than six seconds the swimmer will waste energy lifting the head too often. Holding the breath longer than ten seconds will probably cause most swimmers to gasp for air. Swimmers should feel they have blown out about half their air when they exhale. The amount of air inhaled and exhaled along with breath-holding time must be adjusted until swimmers feel comfortable with the exchange of air.

Stroke

With the hands tilted about 45 degrees, palms outward, swimmers develop a lift force with only a gentle sideward and circular downward movement of the arms. The sideward movement of the arms is continued until the arms are opposite the shoulders. As the hands pass slightly behind the shoulders they face downward until the arms reach the sides of the body. The arm and leg action must be forceful enough to support the head above the water, but should not lift the shoulders above the surface. After swimmers become proficient they can reduce the stroke to a small circular action with the hands kept in front of the body. The trunk should remain angled slightly forward throughout the entire stroke. Even a slight extension of the back will cause the swimmer to sink. If the back is straightened completely when the head is lifted for air, the swimmer will sink well below the surface.

Coordination

The head must remain downward before a breath is taken until the arms are lifted and the wrists crossed in front of the head. Then the head is lifted during exhalation (people of low positive buoyancy should not blow out until the nose and mouth are close to the surface). As the chin emerges the wide sweeping stroke is begun. The shoulders should remain within an inch of the surface during the entire cycle of breathing and floating. If all movement is timed properly with the

Drownproofing

breathing, and the trunk kept angled forward, there will be no bobbing or necessity for a second stroke.

Kicking

Some swimmers feel a light kick is essential to keep the body in balance. After the knees are bent slightly, the feet separate 24 to 28 inches apart forward and backward. This action is done as the arms are lifted toward the surface. The legs are brought together during the armstroke.

ANGLE FLOAT
FOR AVERAGE FLOATERS

A. *Floating position: back of neck at surface. Arms and legs hang loosely downward; hands are under the shoulders and feet under the hips. This position is held for six to ten seconds.*

B. *When swimmer is ready to breathe, arms are lifted toward surface as legs begin to spread. Head is stationary during arm lift.*

C. Wrists are crossed in front of head. Exhalation begins as head is lifted.

D. As chin clears water, arms stroke sideward with palms tilted 45 degrees outward. Legs move toward one another. Trunk remains angled forward. Swimmer inhales during arm stroke.

E. After inhalation, arms circle backward as face is put in water. Legs are brought together.

F. Swimmer returns to floating position.

Practice

Downproof floating should be practiced until a swimmer can float for at least an hour. When tested, people who completed an hour of floating were able to continue for several hours without difficulty. Swimmers should try the angle float with legs crossed using arms only and with hands clasped behind their backs using legs only. This type of practice enables swimmers to appreciate the contribution of body buoyancy to reduction of energy loss. They also realize they can float if afflicted with muscle cramps or injury to limbs.

Points to Remember:

1. Trunk remains angled forward throughout the cycle of floating and breathing.

2. Head stays down until arms are lifted and crossed in front of head.

3. To get air, first lift arms, then tilt head upward, then start stroke.

4. Stroke starts after nose is above surface and continues until bottom of chin is level with surface.

5. Only one arm stroke and one kick are required for each breath.

6. During the floating cycle the head is tilted from a horizontal to a vertical position and then back to the horizontal without altering the angled position of the trunk.

7. While floating, the back of neck is at the surface.

8. Float 6 to 10 seconds between breaths.

VERTICAL FLOAT

Many good floaters cannot perform the angle float because their bodies float in a horizontal position when relaxed. This places them in an awkward position for getting air. Good floaters usually use the vertical float. Good floaters who can easily lift their heads for air while near the horizontal prefer the angle float.

The arm stroke and kick are the same as done when performing the angle float. Only two or three inches of lift is needed to obtain air. The body is kept in a vertical position while floating motionless.

Stroke and Breathing

After a deep breath is taken good floaters sink to their natural floating level with arms at sides. When five or six seconds have passed the arms are raised thumbs up in front of the body until the forearms are crossed in front of the face. With the hands tilted 45 degrees, palms outward, the arms move sideward until the hands are level with the shoulders. As the hands move sideward the body lifts upward while the swimmer exhales. Exhalation is continued until the nose and mouth clear the surface. Inhalation begins as the hands pass behind the shoulders and start downward. During the downward action of the arms the palms face the bottom until the arms are at the sides of the body.

Kicking

A kick is performed to keep the body in a vertical position. After the knees bend, the feet separate 24 to 28 inches apart forward and backward. The legs separate while the arms move upward and are brought together when the arms stroke sideward.

After good floaters are able to float for an hour they should practice the vertical float with legs crossed, and then with their hands clasped behind their backs.

VERTICAL FLOAT FOR GOOD FLOATERS

A. The body floats vertically at natural floating level for six to ten seconds.

B. When swimmer is ready for a breath, arms are raised toward surface as legs begin to spread.

C. *Arms cross in front of face, palms are tilted outward. Legs spread with knees bent.*

D. *Arms move sideward as legs are gently brought together. This action lifts body until chin is level with surface. Swimmer exhales slowly during lift.*

E. *Swimmer inhales as arms stroke sideward and legs are brought together. Bottom of chin is at surface.*

F. Arms pass slightly behind shoulders, then move downward with palms facing the pool bottom.

G. Swimmer returns to vertical float position with body held erect.

Points to Remember:

1. Keep head and trunk erect at all times.

2. Exhale at beginning of arm stroke as body starts to rise.

3. Exhalation continues until nose and mouth are out of water. Shoulders should not rise above surface.

4. For good floaters body needs to rise only two to three inches.

5. Inhalation begins as hands pass behind shoulders at the end of the sideward sweep of the arms.

6. Legs separate as arms lift upward and are brought together during armstroke.

7. Float 6 to 10 seconds between breaths.

3: Drownproof Swimming

Students should be taught drownproof swimming (*travel stroke*) along with drownproof floating. The main emphasis is on a long, simultaneous 180-degree pull of both arms followed by a rest period while the body is balanced and relaxed in a natural floating position. Breathing is separated from propulsion.

There are three variations to the travel stroke, for swimmers of the three different buoyancy types. The *average floater* uses a scissor kick, executed in the vertical plane, which offers support and levels the body to the horizontal. *Good floaters* keep their legs near the surface by doing a lateral spread kick. *Sinkers* do not allow their legs to go below a 45-degree angle from the horizontal. When performed correctly, the travel stroke allows a swimmer to progress about one mile per hour.

REGULAR TRAVEL STROKE
FOR AVERAGE FLOATERS

From a prone face-down position with arms extended along the surface beyond the head the swimmer presses backward and downward against the water with both hands. The body moves forward until the thighs are even with the hands. The swimmer then relaxes completely and allows the arms and legs to drop to the natural floating position. The arms are then lifted toward the surface as the legs begin to spread. Head remains stationary until the wrists are crossed in front of the head. Air is exhaled while the head is lifted out of water. A short sideward stroke along with a kick is taken while the swimmer inhales air. After air is inhaled the head is dropped back in the water as the arms circle backward and around until extended beyond the head. One foot is raised to the surface while the other leg stays vertical. A second kick is used to level the body to the horizontal, after which another long stroke is begun.

The travel stroke consists of a long stroke and a glide followed by a short stroke and a breath. The average floater moves from the horizontal to a semi-vertical floating position for a breath and back to the horizontal position for travel. The body returns to its natural floating position for relaxation after each long stroke.

REGULAR TRAVEL STROKE
FOR AVERAGE FLOATERS

A. *Swimmer starts in horizontal position with arms extended forward.*

B. *Swimmer moves arms through 180 degrees sideward and backward.*

C. *A glide follows the long double arm pull.*

D. *Legs and arms are allowed to drop and relax, as body settles to a natural floating position.*

E. Arms pass through natural floating position and are lifted toward surface.

F. As arms are lifted toward surface, palms facing one another, legs move apart.

G. Arms are crossed in front of head as legs spread.

H. Swimmer exhales as head is tilted upward. When chin clears surface, swimmer inhales; arms stroke sideward and legs are brought together.

I. Arms circle backward, and head is dropped back into water.

J. As arms circle downward, one foot is raised toward surface.

K. *Arms are raised toward surface.*

L. *Arms are extended beyond head. One leg is near surface, while other leg dangles downward.*

M. *A scissor kick is performed by bringing legs together, to move body to horizontal position. Arms are ready to start another long travel stroke.*

Points to Remember:

1. The body is allowed to settle to a natural floating position (angle float) at the completion of the long arm stroke.

2. The arm, leg, and head movements for getting air are the same as for the angle float.

3. A scissor kick in the vertical plane is done to level the body to the horizontal before the long travel stroke is started.

4. A full cycle of the travel stroke is completed in six to ten seconds.

5. A swimmer travels about one mile per hour when performing the travel stroke.

HORIZONTAL TRAVEL STROKE
FOR GOOD FLOATERS

Since it would take considerable effort to force their legs under their bodies, good floaters allow their legs to float in a horizontal position when they perform the travel stroke. Sinkers of high negative buoyancy find it advantageous to use this variation of the travel stroke. The arm action of the travel stroke for good floaters is identical to the arm action of the travel stroke for average floaters. A lateral spread kick is used to balance the body by slightly bending the knees and separating the legs sideward to about the width of the shoulders. The knees are then straightened as the legs are brought together.

A. *Swimmer begins with body in horizontal position and arms extended beyond head with face in water.*

B. *Arms are pressed sideward and backward through an arc of 180 degrees.*

C. When hands are at thighs, swimmer glides and completely relaxes arms and legs.

D. Arms are allowed to drop and move through vertical toward surface.

E. *Arms cross in front of head as legs spread laterally.*

F. *Head is tilted upward until bottom of chin is at surface. A short stroke is performed as air is inhaled. Shoulders are slightly behind hands at end of stroke. A lateral spread kick is done by bending knees and moving legs sideward to about width of shoulders.*

G. Head is dropped back in water while arms move forward (thumbs leading) to extended position beyond head as legs are brought together.

Points to Remember

1. The entire body of a good floater when relaxed floats at or near the horizontal.

2. The swimmer relaxes at the end of long travel stroke and allows head, arms, and legs to float. (Wrinkles in back of neck during the glide are a sign that the head is being held too high.)

3. Arms then move forward through the vertical plane (palms facing one another) to beyond the head.

4. Feet are spread laterally (about the width of the hips) to maintain balance just before head is lifted for air.

SINKER'S TRAVEL STROKE
FOR THE NONBUOYANT

Swimmers whose negative buoyancy does not allow them to float motionless use the sinker's travel stroke. The travel stroke for "sinkers" is identical to the regular travel stroke for average floaters but sinkers must not allow their legs to sink below 45 degrees from horizontal. Sinkers should expend just enough effort to keep themselves within 45 degrees of the surface.

Sinkers who possess high negative buoyancy usually prefer the lateral spread kick used by good floaters. This lateral movement keeps the legs closer to the surface than does the scissor kick done in the vertical plane.

Because their bodies are more buoyant in salt water than in fresh water many sinkers find that in ocean water they can use the floating and swimming techniques designed for average floaters.

Breathing Drill for Sinkers

Sinkers practice breathing by holding on to the rung of a ladder or other support about one foot below the water surface. With feet on the bottom and the body held in an inclined position, face in water, the sinker can practice breathing by alternately tilting the head upward and downward.

BREATHING DRILL FOR SINKERS

Swimmer grasps support one foot below surface. With feet on bottom, face in water, and body held in an inclined position, swimmer practices breathing by alternately tilting head upward and downward.

A. *Swimmer begins in face-down horizontal position with arms extended beyond head.*

B. *Arms press sideward and backward toward thighs.*

C. When hands reach thighs, swimmer glides and relaxes completely.

D. Arms and legs are allowed to drop. When legs reach 45 degrees below the horizontal, arms move toward surface.

E. *Arms cross in front of head as one foot moves toward surface.*

F. *Swimmer exhales just before nose and mouth break the surface. Swimmer inhales while performing a short sideward arm stroke and bringing legs together.*

G. *Arms circle backward and downward as head is dropped back into water. One leg is raised toward surface.*

H. *Arms are lifted to surface and extended beyond head. One leg is near surface while other leg dangles downward.*

I. A scissor kick is done by bringing legs together, which moves the body back to a horizontal position.

Points to Remember:

1. A sinker completes a cycle of the stroke once every four to six seconds.

2. A sinker relaxes after the long stroke until the legs drop to about 45 degrees from the surface.

3. A sinker does not exhale until nose and mouth are near the surface.

4: Drownproofing for Nonswimmers

The drownproofing method is extremely helpful to unskilled swimmers and nonswimmers. Thousands of nonswimmers, after learning these techniques, have been able to swim long distances and float for long periods. Some swimming specialists feel that drownproofing is an advanced set of techniques best taught only to those who are able to perform regular swimming strokes. Others believe the use of drownproofing techniques should be limited to emergency situations. However, there is much merit in the idea that these techniques ought to be the first skills learned by *everyone.*

TEACHING INFANTS TO SWIM

For the past several years there have been a number of authorities around the country who have discouraged swimming instruction for infants under three years of age. There were a number of reasons, they said, that infants could not learn. One of the main reasons set forth was that an infant's neck musculature was not strong enough to lift the head above the surface to get air. Another was the suggestion that infants lacked judgment and might put themselves in unsafe situations.

There are many cases of children under the age of three swimming and learning to swim. They were able to swim ten or twelve feet underwater, but then had to emerge when they needed a breath, at which time the swimming stopped. While conducting a drownproofing seminar in Honolulu, I met Mary Ann Sears, who has been teaching infants to swim over the past twenty-five years. She has been able to train infants, during the initial stages of instruction through a paddling action of arms and legs, to rotate their bodies backward from a horizontal or semi-horizontal to a vertical position. With their bodies vertical infants can get air by tilting their heads backward. While inhaling, the back of the infant's head is in the water. They then return themselves to the horizontal position and continue swimming. This procedure places no stress whatsoever on the neck musculature. All the infants taught by Mary Ann Sears were able to swim around a pool several times, and far exceeded the limitations, of the ten- or twelve-foot swim, observed for other infants. Under her supervision, infants were able to get repeated exchanges of air; they were not just swimming underwater, but surfaced for air many times while swimming. These observations firmly convinced me that *with qualified and experienced instruction*, infants can learn to swim. (Without qualified instruction, however, infants will benefit from exposure to water, though they will probably not learn how to swim until a later age.) Infants must be put in relatively warm water nearly every day before they can learn to swim. One thing in the infants' favor is that unless malnourished, they are all positively buoyant and, therefore, will float while motionless.

According to Mary Ann Sears, infants show more judgment than some authorities are willing to admit. She described one occasion when an infant tried to emerge from the pool and was not able to do so because the water surface was too far below the deck level. The infant kept swimming around until she found the steps, and she was able to crawl out. In another instance, an infant was shown how to go to the bottom of a pool six feet beneath the surface and put three rings on one arm and two rings on another. The infant, only six months old, accomplished this feat with no difficulty whatsoever!

It does appear that teaching swimming to infants is something that should be further explored. If parents feel it is advantageous for their infants to learn how to swim they ought to seek out competent instructors. But one has to proceed with caution in this regard and consider the advantages of a child learning to swim before age three. Certainly there are many advantages to being exposed to the water environment, at any age. Repeated exposure will enhance familiarity with the water. Children who have had frequent exposure to the water will learn swimming more quickly than those who have had little or no exposure.

The techniques of drownproofing are particularly applicable to infants learning to swim. Infants naturally float with their faces in the water once they have learned to hold their breath underwater. This means that the simultaneous action of the arms used in both the floating and travel stroke can be used by infants very effectively. The periodic emergence for air coincides with the Mary Ann Sears method of having infants rotate around and get their air by simply tilting their heads backward. The principle of drownproofing applies because infants are able to use body buoyancy to conserve energy.

MOTIVATION OF NONSWIMMERS

Most nonswimmers are afraid of the water, regardless of their age. The main thing an instructor must do is provide situations which tend to reduce this fear. Some children will not cooperate with an instructor because they have no desire to do something which they think will be unpleasant, such as putting their faces in water. Other times they refuse because they fear water and the possibility of choking.

Parents who give in to children who will not undergo an unpleasant experience will be dissatisfied with the results achieved by most swimming instructors. Certainly, children must be given clear and concise instruction, but the instructor must be firm. Children must be *told*, not asked, to perform certain tasks. Submerging their faces may seem unpleasant at the outset, but it can be easily demonstrated by an instructor that no harm will come to them if they follow a few easy steps. Learners should be instructed to take a deep breath, hold it, seal their mouths tightly with their lips, and then put their faces in the water. Secondly, they are to repeat this procedure, but as they lift their heads above the water, exhale slowly through their noses until their chins clear the surface. Finally, they submerge their faces for five or six seconds, exhale as they tilt their heads upward, take a breath and put their faces back in the water. These procedures are relatively simple and children should be impelled to complete these fundamentals. Proper instruction in breathing and breath control will guard against choking.

The introduction to deep water for a nonswimmer should be taught early in the instruction, even on the first or second day. This can be done with a plastic line, or with the instructor assisting the nonswimmer while both are in the water. Too much time spent swimming in shallow water unquestionably denies the nonswimmer the experience of real swimming. No one will ever learn to be safe in deep water while swimming in shallow water. With use of a plastic line to help support the nonswimmer when necessary, learners will soon experience being suspended in deep water well above the bottom of a pool, which is a new revelation to them. Many nonswimmers comment on how high up they feel they are above the bottom of the pool while floating or swimming.

Each nonswimmer, when learning drownproofing techniques, should experience marked progress. It should be made clear to them how much longer they floated on the second day than on the first. A two-minute float on the third day can be turned into five minutes on the fourth, fifteen minutes on the fifth, and half an hour on the sixth day. During these same sessions, the actual swimming distance should be measured. Thirty feet on the first day, a length of the pool on the second day, around the pool on the third, two hundred yards on the fourth day. A consistent effort should be made to encourage the nonswimmer to double and triple his distance each day thereafter until a mile is completed. Students must be made aware of repeated improvements to feel the influence of success.

Most swimming instructors favor teaching the crawl stroke to beginners—probably because of the popularity of this stroke in competitive swimming. But questions must be asked: Should not people be able to stay at the surface with minimal expenditure of energy before they learn to swim fast? Would it not be better to teach a restful gentle stroke first than a racing stroke? Even the side and breast strokes do not allow the relaxation experienced by a swimmer who performs the travel stroke. The position of complete extension held by a swimmer during the glide phase of the breast and side strokes does not compare to the relaxed natural floating position of the travel stroke.

The first aim for nonswimmers is to feel safe in the water; to be able to swim and float in a relaxed, easy manner without stress or struggle. They must learn how to hold their breath underwater, exhale underwater, and repeatedly to get an exchange of air. Conscious breath control is an important factor because buoyancy is affected by the amount of air in the lungs. Few people have enough buoyancy to float or swim while holding their heads above the surface. Swimmers waste valuable energy when they try to keep their heads out of water. Exertion can be reduced to a minimum if the body is allowed to float at its natural floating level. After nonswimmers learn to use body buoyancy to conserve energy *they find* floating and swimming requires no more effort than walking.

A word of warning: unskilled and nonswimmers should learn drownproofing techniques only in the presence of an instructor.

BREATHING STANDING DRILL

Nonswimmers begin by standing in chest deep water facing the pool wall. After they grasp the gutter with both hands and inhale deeply they submerge their heads for three or four seconds. Trials are repeated until everyone can stay under for six seconds. The mouth is kept tightly closed when under the surface. While underwater, nonswimmers can acquaint themselves with their surroundings. They should keep their eyes open and look around. Although vision is blurred they are able to see their feet, walls of the pool, lines on the bottom, and become aware of the under surface of the water. Everyone must be able to distinguish whether the water surface is at brow level or above the head. Use of swimmers' goggles are recommended because they improve underwater vision, eliminate eye irritation, and increase depth perception.

The next thing to learn is how to blow out in the water. A deep breath is taken, then with the mouth tightly closed (sealed by the lips) the head is submerged for six seconds. As the head emerges air is exhaled forcibly and steadily through the nose until the chin is out of water. Exhalation must take place only on the way up, not on the way down and must be continued until the nose and mouth are clear of the water. (Nonswimmers should feel they are blowing out about half the air in their lungs.) Inhalation is done through the mouth.

The mouth is kept tightly closed when under the surface. Exhalation is through the nose as the head emerges.

BREATHING FLOAT DRILL
FOR AVERAGE FLOATERS

Beginners who are average floaters hold the gutter with one hand while the body is angled forward. The free arm and legs dangle loosely downward. After a deep breath is taken the head is tilted downward into the water. The breath is held for six seconds. Exhalation begins as the head is tilted upward and is continued until the nose and mouth are above the surface. Inhalation begins after drops of water have been blown away from the nose and mouth. When inhalation is complete the head is tilted downward into the water.

BREATHING FLOAT DRILL
FOR GOOD FLOATERS

Good floaters practice breathing by holding on to the gutter with thumbs only. The entire body is pressed against the wall with knees bent 90 degrees, arms stretched sideward and feet clear of bottom. The drill should be continued until nonswimmers can alternately inhale and exhale about ten times without a hitch. The breath should be held for six to ten seconds—long enough to allow for an appreciable rest period but short enough to prevent gasping for air.

HORIZONTAL BREATHING DRILL FOR
SINKERS, AVERAGE AND
GOOD FLOATERS

Some nonswimmers find it easier to practice breathing while the body is at or near the horizontal rather than the vertical position. Hands may be placed on the gutter, ladder, or steps of a pool. The head is tilted upward as air is exhaled. After air is inhaled the head is tilted downward and the face is submerged. The breath is held for six to ten seconds. Sinkers perform this drill with feet on bottom and the body held in an inclined position.

BREATHING STROKE DRILL
FOR AVERAGE FLOATERS

Nonswimmers who are average floaters can combine a stroking movement with breathing by holding on to the gutter with one hand. With the body angled forward, face in water the free arm is lifted and crossed in front of the head. Air is exhaled as the head is tilted upward. Inhalation occurs when the chin is level with the surface and the free arm (hand tilted

45 degrees, palm outward) is stroked gently sideward and downward.

BREATHING STROKE DRILL
FOR GOOD FLOATERS

Good floaters start by holding the gutter with one hand. The body is held in a vertical position side to the wall. After a deep breath is taken the body is allowed to sink to the natural floating level. The breath is held for five or six seconds. The free arm is then raised and crossed in front of the face as the legs separate. Exhalation is begun as the free arm strokes sideward. When the free arm has moved through a 90 degree angle inhalation begins and continues until the arm circles backward behind the shoulder and downward. The legs are brought together as the body returns to its natural floating level.

SUPPORT LINE

Nonswimmers can be introduced to deep water with the use of a plastic line, one end of which is tied around the learner's waist and the other end held by an instructor. This procedure has been extremely successful because the instructor controls the tension in the line. Nonswimmers are able to experiment

HORIZONTAL BREATHING DRILL

A. Position for horizontal breathing float drill for average and good floaters.

B. Position for breathing stroke drill for average floaters.

C. Position for breathing stroke drill for good floaters.

with body buoyancy until they realize air and water will keep them afloat. After nonswimmers have demonstrated they can either do the angle or vertical float for five minutes they are ready to practice without the aid of a line. Floating practice should be continued until everyone can float for an hour in deep water.

Use of support line is helpful to nonswimmer in deep water.

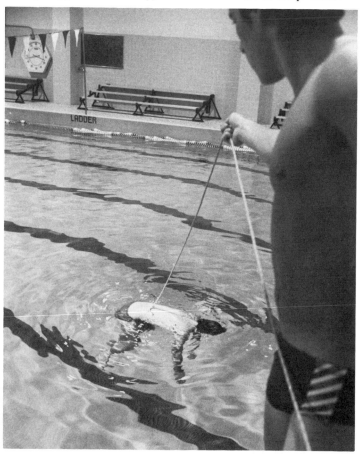

ELEMENTARY TRAVEL STROKE

During sessions on breathing and floating nonswimmers can also learn how to move through the water. The nonbuoyant, who cannot float motionless, must start to learn the travel stroke following practice of breathing drills.

Standing up from Prone Float

Nonswimmers must be able to stand up in shallow water following a prone face-down float. Standing in chest-deep water, the swimmer takes a deep breath, and lowers the

STANDING UP FROM PRONE FLOAT

A. Nonswimmer begins by standing in chest deep water, takes a deep breath, lowers shoulders under water and extends arms forward.

shoulders underwater. The body is allowed to lean slowly forward until the feet leave the bottom, then lies as flat as possible at the surface with the arms extended beyond the head. During the first few trials an instructor may help to support the body. Arms and legs are spread slightly sideward to maintain balance. Standing is accomplished by pressing the arms downward and backward to the thighs while at the same time bending the knees until the feet are firmly placed on the bottom. Air is exhaled as the head is lifted above the surface. Before starting again, air is inhaled. The entire drill is repeated with a gentle push off the bottom. The body is allowed to glide along the surface before being brought to a standing position.

B. After face is in water, nonswimmer pushes gently from bottom.

STANDING UP FROM PRONE FLOAT *cont.*

C. *After a gentle push from bottom, the body reaches a prone float position.*

Drownproofing

D. To stand up, nonswimmer presses downward and backward with arms and brings legs under body.

STANDING UP FROM PRONE FLOAT *cont.*

E. *After feet are placed firmly on the bottom, air is exhaled as head is raised.*

Drownproofing

F. Air is inhaled before nonswimmer starts again.

ELEMENTARY TRAVEL STROKE—
STROKING AND STANDING

A. After push from the bottom, body glides to a face-down horizontal position with arms extended beyond head.

Stroking and Standing

After standing in chest-deep water the nonswimmer pushes from the bottom and glides face down in the extended position. Palms are tilted slightly outward as arms and hands press sideward and backward until the hands reach the thighs. The arms are allowed to drop below the body, then reach forward beyond the head. Arms press downward and backward as the nonswimmer comes to a standing position. This procedure is repeated until the nonswimmer can cover about sixty feet without hesitation.

B. When body is in prone float, nonswimmer performs a long
   travel stroke.

C. Travel stroke ends with hands at thighs.

D. *After a short glide, arms and legs are dropped.*

E. Arms are moved near surface as legs continue to drop.

F. Arms are pressed backward as feet are placed on bottom.

G. *Air is exhaled as head is lifted*

H. After head emerges, air is inhaled as swimmer prepares to repeat the sequence.

Stroking

A long stroke must be followed by a short stroke. The short stroke is completed when the shoulders pass the hands. Before each short stroke, air is exhaled, and the head tilted upward. Air is then inhaled and the head is tilted downward into the water while the arms reach forward. All movements are made slowly and gently.

Stroking and Leg Action

Following a push off the bottom, glide, and a simultaneous backward stroke with the arms, both legs are allowed to sink about three feet below the surface. The knees are bent slightly as one foot is brought near the surface. This kicking action is accomplished by moving the foot of one leg downward as the foot of the other leg moves upward. One kick is performed as the head emerges for air and is followed by a second kick just after the head is put back in the water.

A good floater will prefer to kick by separating the legs sideward as the knees bend. The feet are brought together when the legs are straightened. This style of kicking offers little propulsion but keeps the body in balance.

Tether Swimming

Many beginners have learned to swim the travel stroke in a relatively short time by allowing an instructor to guide them with a plastic line one end of which is tied around the beginner's waist. While the instructor controls the tension in the line, the beginner is able to determine the amount of horizontal motion necessary to stay at the surface. With this type of tether a beginner can practice the stroke in deep water.

Distance should be increased with each trial. After a beginner can cover 100 yards in deep water with a tether line, the line should no longer be used. At this point some beginners find it helpful to have an instructor swim alongside a few times. The travel stroke should be practiced until a beginner can swim one mile.

ELEMENTARY TRAVEL STROKE— BREATHING

Nonswimmer replaces standing up with short breathing stroke.

ELEMENTARY TRAVEL STROKE—
LEG ACTION

A. One leg kick is performed with the short stroke to support
the body while head is out of water.

B. A second kick is performed after inhalation to level body to
the horizontal just before the long travel stroke.

A line supports swimmer while breathing techniques are learned.

4: Drownproofing for Nonswimmers   *117*

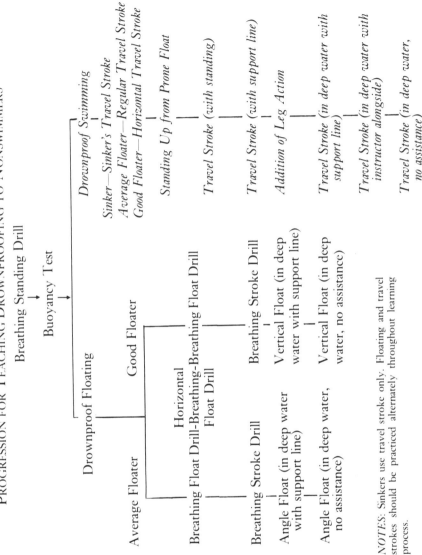

PROGRESSION FOR TEACHING DROWNPROOFING TO NONSWIMMERS

Breathing Standing Drill

Buoyancy Test

Drownproof Floating

Drownproof Swimming

Sinker—Sinker's Travel Stroke
Average Floater—Regular Travel Stroke
Good Floater—Horizontal Travel Stroke

Standing Up from Prone Float

Travel Stroke (with standing)

Travel Stroke (with support line)

Addition of Leg Action

Travel Stroke (in deep water with support line)

Travel Stroke (in deep water with instructor alongside)

Travel Stroke (in deep water, no assistance)

Average Floater

Good Floater

Horizontal
Breathing Float Drill–Breathing–Breathing Float Drill Float Drill

Breathing Stroke Drill

Breathing Stroke Drill

Angle Float (in deep water with support line)

Vertical Float (in deep water with support line)

Angle Float (in deep water, no assistance)

Vertical Float (in deep water, no assistance)

NOTES: Sinkers use travel stroke only. Floating and travel strokes should be practiced alternately throughout learning process.

118

Drownproofing

AIDS TO LEARNING

No two individuals will learn a skill in the same way because of differences in ability and past experience. However, the suggestions presented below may be helpful. They arise from observation of hundreds of people as they practiced drownproofing techniques.

Mental Picture

Swimmers must have a clear idea of the drownproofing technique they are about to practice. A mental picture can be attained by watching another swimmer, a film of the technique, or a study of instructions and diagrams.

Whole vs. Part

After learning the breathing drills, concentration should be directed to the whole floating stroke rather than to the parts. The continuity of motion must be understood from beginning to end. For correction or refinement of technique, the parts can be practiced in subsequent trials.

Awareness

Performance of a technique requires both movement and thought. Once the concept of buoyancy is understood no one will harbor the idea that water pulls them under. To gain a feel for the water, swimmers must be consciously aware of the application of force and the extent to which force is used for support and propulsion.

Practice

Daily practice is essential during the initial stages. A lapse of two or three days between sessions will slow down the learning process and may bring it to a standstill. Each session should last an hour. As soon as a technique can be repeated a few times, a continuous effort of five to ten minutes duration is soon accomplished. Floating time and distance swimming should increase each day. All practice time is spent in the water. Drills on land are practically worthless. The unique quality of the water environment, which gives a feeling of weightlessness, precludes all notions that movements practiced on land simulate those made in water.

5: A Drownproofing Program

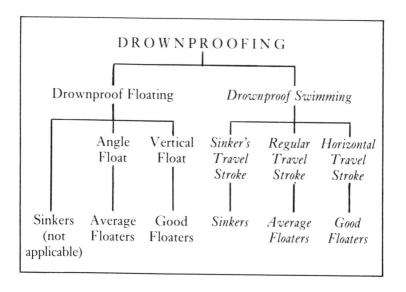

DROWNPROOFING

Drownproof Floating   *Drownproof Swimming*

Angle Float   Vertical Float   *Sinker's Travel Stroke*   *Regular Travel Stroke*   *Horizontal Travel Stroke*

Sinkers (not applicable)   Average Floaters   Good Floaters   *Sinkers*   *Average Floaters*   *Good Floaters*

People who can swim 50 yards or more are able to learn all the drownproofing techniques in four to six one-hour sessions. Unskilled and nonswimmers usually require eight to twelve sessions. A few may require 18 to 30 hours. The main objectives are for everyone to float one hour and swim one mile. This program has been used in many elementary, junior and senior high schools, colleges, camps, and recreation centers. The numbers in a class should be limited: ten to each instructor. Separate sections should be arranged for swimmers and nonswimmers.

FIRST SESSION:
Introduction to Drownproofing

(LECTURE) *If you were cast from a boat into rough water while fully clad and after a few minutes muscles in two limbs were afflicted with cramps, you would surely want to know the best techniques for staying alive in the water.*

These techniques are available to you in the form of drownproof floating and drownproof swimming and will enable you to stay at or near the surface, if the water is warm enough, for a long period. If you can do these techniques in a lake or ocean you will be able to drift with moving water to shore or float until rescued.

But mastery of drownproofing techniques is not all there is to drownproofing. The second part is learning how to control panic.

Many drowning accidents are due to panic and you will never be safe in the water until you learn to get out of trouble.

The techniques you learn in this course are designed to keep you alive while floating and swimming fully clothed in a rough sea, even when afflicted with muscle cramps.

(DEMONSTRATION) *The Limitations of Basic Swimming Skills for Water Survival.*

TREADING WATER AND MOTIONLESS FLOAT

A. Treading water.

Treading Water. Treading with the head above water is good for momentary orientation, but because of the continuous motion of arms and legs, it uses three times more energy than drownproof floating. Demonstrator shows the treading action with head above water, then takes a deep breath and floats motionless in the angle and vertical float position.

B. Motionless float.

Back Floating and Swimming.   Horizontal back floating can be performed by only highly buoyant individuals—most people float at a 45 degree to a 60 degree angle from the horizontal. A swimmer who completely relaxes will rotate from the back float to the face-down angle float position. In rough water waves wash over the faces of people who swim on their backs. Demonstrator shows how the body rotates from the position of backfloating to the face-down angle float, and points out the vulnerable position of the nostrils when in a backfloat position.

Crawl Stroke.   The crawl stroke is designed for speed and works well for marathon or competitive swimmers in good condition. But buoyancy is reduced when the arms are lifted out of water which soon tires the untrained average swimmer.

Drownproof Floating

(LECTURE) *If you fill your lungs with air and sink to your natural floating level, air and water will keep you afloat. Before you submerge close your mouth tightly and if you are an average floater angle your trunk forward 45 degrees from vertical. Let your head float and limbs hang loosely downward. The entire body must be relaxed to allow your built-in life preserver, namely, your lungs, to keep you afloat. About every six to ten seconds you lift your head for air. If this technique is done correctly the shoulders will remain at the surface while only the head tilts upward and downward. If you prefer the vertical float you should keep your trunk in an erect position while lifting the body for air.*

(DEMONSTRATION) Demonstrator performs buoyancy test, angle and vertical floating techniques. Breathing float drills and breathing stroke drills are then explained and demonstrated. Emphasis is placed on the sideward sweeping armstroke with palms tilted outward.

Practice. Everyone tries the buoyancy test to determine his or her body type: good floater, average floater, or nonbuoyant. Students then practice the breathing float drills and breathing stroke drills. During these drills the instructor reminds students to keep their mouths tightly closed while submerged. Water must be exhaled through the nose only while the head emerges. Exhalation must be slow, gradual, and controlled. If water enters the mouth it can be expectorated beneath the surface through tight lips.

Average floaters practice the angle float. Good floaters do either angle or vertical float. The nonbuoyant must be shown the sinker's travel stroke.

Safety Precautions. Some unskilled swimmers may be reluctant to perform drownproof floating for extended periods. Instructors must convince these students that learning will be successful only by persistence. However, an instructor must be constantly aware of a swimmer's reaction—two missed breaths mean difficulty. A verbal exchange between instructor and swimmer is essential when difficulty arises. While breaths are taken by a swimmer the instructor must discern whether or not there is a proper exchange of air. Some swimmers tend to swallow air; others fail to breathe in air even when they appear to inhale. Swimmers should continue to practice only after their difficulties have been analyzed.

SECOND SESSION:
Swimming Fully Clothed
and Travel Strokes

(LECTURE) *Heavy wet masses have tremendous intertial lag and must be moved slowly through the water. Arms and legs covered with clothes must be recovered slowly and should never be lifted from the water. The crawl or overarm sidestroke are almost useless if a swimmer is in a rough sea while fully clad. On the other hand, in cold water a swimmer should not disrobe because clothes, by trapping air next to the skin, triple survival time.*

(DEMONSTRATION) Demonstrator shows the regular travel stroke by starting with the angle float position to point out that the travel stroke is an extension of the angle float. Emphasis is placed on the intermediate position where the swimmer has arms pointed forward, face in water, one leg pointed downward and the foot of the other leg near the surface. It should be mentioned there are two scissor kicks done in the vertical plane per cycle of stroke: one kick is performed to level the body to the horizontal, the second kick helps to support the body while the head is above water to get air.

Demonstration of the sinker's and horizontal travel stroke begins with the swimmer in the horizontal position. Sinkers do not allow their legs to sink below 45 degrees after the long travel stroke, and good floaters keep near the horizontal throughout the stroke cycle.

PRACTICE:

New—Swimmers travel stroke around pool.

Review—Drownproof floating.

A. Drownproof floating fully clothed — back of head is at surface.

B. Travel stroke fully clothed.

T H I R D   S E S S I O N : Muscle Cramps—
Floating and Swimming with Two Limbs

(LECTURE) *A muscle cramp is usually due to fatigue. Frequently, cramps occur in the calf of the leg or bottom of the foot. On occasion, canoeists who paddle for long periods or sailors who remain in a fixed position, when suddenly cast overboard experience multiple cramps in which two limbs are afflicted. A swimmer can always remove a cramp by stretching the afflicted muscle. For example, a cramp in the calf of the leg can be relieved by extending the leg at the knee joint and raising the foot toward the shin. Usually a cramp is preceded by a warning twinge which gives the swimmer time to stop and float before onset of the cramp. After swimmers remove cramps they should float and rest for a few minutes. Most cramps will recur if swimmers attempt to use the afflicted limbs immediately. Drownproof floating and drownproof swimming are particularly helpful techniques to swimmers afflicted with cramps. The angle or vertical float position may be used while a swimmer stretches the afflicted limb. Swimmers may easily float and swim without the use of two limbs when they use drownproofing techniques.*

(DEMONSTRATION) *Floating and Swimming with Two Limbs.*
1. Angle float and vertical float using arms only and using legs only.
2. All variations of the travel stroke using arms only followed by use of legs only.

PRACTICE:
New—Float and swim with legs crossed in Buddha fashion.
Float and swim with hands held behind back.

Review—Drownproof floating and travel stroke. Practice floating for 15 to 20 minutes and travel stroke for 400–500 yards.

F O U R T H   S E S S I O N : Floating Test

Float one hour while wearing long-sleeved shirt, long pants, and sneakers. The nonbuoyant or sinkers do not perform the floating test.

F I F T H   S E S S I O N : Distance Swim

Travel stroke one mile wearing long-sleeved shirt, pants, and sneakers. Swimmers may stop and drownproof float at any time during the swim. Sinkers swim one mile and continue until in water for one hour.

S I X T H   S E S S I O N : Test on Floating and Swimming with Two Limbs

1. Float 10 minutes and swim travel stroke 100 yards with legs crossed in Buddha style. (Sinkers do travel stroke with arms only.)
2. Float 10 minutes and swim travel stroke with hands held behind back. (Sinkers do travel stroke with legs only.)

A. *Angle float with legs crossed.*

B. Arms are lifted toward surface.

C. Wrists are crossed in front of head.

D. *Swimmer exhales as head is tilted upward. Swimmer inhales while arms perform a short sideward stroke.*

E. *Swimmer returns to angle float by circling arms backward and downward and dropping head back into water.*

A. Angle float with hands clasped behind back.

B. *Legs spread before head is lifted. Swimmer begins to exhale.*

C. Exhalation stops when chin is at surface. Legs begin to close as swimmer begins to inhale.

D. *As legs are brought together, swimmer inhales.*

E. Swimmer returns to floating position by tilting head downward into water.

VERTICAL FLOAT—ARMS ONLY

Vertical float with legs crossed.

Vertical float with hands clasped behind back.

REGULAR TRAVEL STROKE—
ARMS ONLY

A. A long stroke is followed by a short stroke.

B. Air is inhaled during short stroke.

REGULAR TRAVEL STROKE—
LEGS ONLY

A. Scissor kick levels body to horizontal, followed by a second scissor kick which moves swimmer forward.

B. Before tilting head upward for air, swimmer spreads legs.

C. *Swimmer exhales as head is tilted upward. Swimmer inhales as legs are brought together.*

D. *Swimmer returns to float position to get ready for another travel stroke kick.*

6: *Application of Drownproofing Techniques*

OPEN WATER SURVIVAL

Ocean and Lake Swimming

If possible, instructors should take students who have completed a drownproofing course to either a lake or ocean because no amount of training in a pool can simulate the conditions of open water. Instructors must check ahead of time for tidal currents, rip tides, and water temperature. Swimmers should swim parallel to the shore with the accompanying boat on the seaward side. An instructor and an associate should be in the boat.

High Waves and Moving Water

The vast array of inland lakes, rivers, ponds and coastal waters provide numerous opportunities for people to engage in open water activities. Open water is readily available to yachtsmen, surfriders, scuba divers, water skiers, and swimmers; seamen and fishermen spend over half their waking hours on the water, yet, when some of these people fully clothed fall overboard and are confronted with long immersion in rough or turbulent water—they may panic and drown. People are warned to "hang on to a boat or canoe if it overturns and wear a lifejacket when boating." Yet boats drift away, people neglect to wear lifejackets, and swimmers overestimate their ability to survive in the water, resulting in loss of life.

A swimmer must learn to drift with moving water alternating the use of drownproof floating with the travel stroke. At all times the swimmer is at the surface, able to get air at will, whether at the crest or hollow of a wave.

Exhaustion

Facts reported about the high incidence of people who drown close to safety or to shore may associate exhaustion as a major cause of drowning. Swimmers and nonswimmers when unexpectedly immersed in deep water make sudden quick attempts to rescue themselves—a procedure which on many occasions results in fatigue. Training in drownproof floating and drownproof swimming conditions swimmers to move slowly and conserve energy.

Various people have experienced the value of drownproofing as a means of self rescue. Many were cast from boats long distances from shore while sailing, fishing, or cruising. Some were picked up after drownproof floating for several hours, others were able to swim back to shore; none complained of exhaustion or muscle fatigue.

Encumbrance of clothes

Many people believe heavy water-logged clothes will drag them under. Rapid movement of arms and legs or lifting limbs above the surface with heavy wet masses on them will soon tire a swimmer. But the encumbrance of clothing can be reduced to a minimum by moving slowly through the water—repeated lungfuls of air keeping the swimmer afloat. The slow gentle motion of the travel stroke coupled with drownproof floating is a very restful and effective combination of movement for the fully-clothed swimmer.

Muscle Cramps

Fatigue of untrained muscles may bring about static contraction or muscle cramps. Usually cramps are preceded by warning twinges. If untreated, cramped muscles may stay knotted for several minutes. Muscle cramps occur most frequently in the calf of the leg or sole of the foot but may appear in the arms, thighs, and abdominal muscles. Fortunately, a cramp can be removed by stretching and massaging the afflicted muscle. For example, if a cramp occurs in the calf muscle of the leg, it can be reduced by extending or straightening the leg and pulling the foot toward the front of the leg. This would be followed by massage of the affected muscle. However, the cramp may recur if the affected limb is used soon after the attack.

Canoeists who have been paddling in a kneeling position and sailors who have been holding a tiller for long periods—if they are cast overboard and try to swim—may undergo an attack of muscle cramps. Those who swim while keeping muscles under tension may also be subjected to cramps.

People may get into trouble when in the water while cramped because of panic. They feel a cramp inhibits them to the point where they can no longer survive. Nothing could be further from the truth. Large numbers of people, all ages, have successfully performed tests of floating and swimming with two or three limbs tied securely (comparable to cramps) while using drownproofing techniques. It is possible to swim and float for long periods with the use of only one or two limbs. Cramps can be removed while in the drownproof floating position. The swimmer is then able to continue to progress through the water with a variation of the travel stroke, using one arm or leg.

Drownproofing techniques are effective unless a swimmer is rendered useless by injury, faced with the thick foam of white water, or held under water—factors which limit the use of all swimming techniques.

Cold Water Immersion

Effects of cold water immersion on swimmers who use drownproofing techniques needs further investigation. Measurements have been restricted to heat loss and do not include the energy cost of work in water. Researchers claim that drownproof floating causes greater heat loss than treading water with the head out of water. However, other studies have shown that treading water requires almost three times more energy than drownproof floating. Total heat loss and energy cost of work should be measured before a comparison is made of water survival techniques. Heat loss and energy expenditure experienced by a swimmer who performs the travel stroke should also be compared to swimmers who use other swimming strokes.

A considerable amount of research has been conducted in the area of cold water immersion. As a result of this research, recommendations, including heat-escape-lessening posture, the huddle technique, and use of seamless thermo jackets, have already become a part of cold water survival instructional programs. Estimated times for cold water survival and the records of surface water temperatures are excellent guides for fishermen, scuba divers, surfers, and swimmers.

However, the situation of individuals immersed in cold water without flotation aids is another matter, particularly if a comparison is made of different floating or swimming techniques. One research team estimated that a swimmer, treading with head held above the surface in water at 50 degrees Fahrenheit, would survive two hours. They also estimated that a swimmer in water at this same temperature who performed drownproof floating would survive one and one-half hours. The difference in survival times was attributed to the additional heat loss by the body, particularly the face and head, when a swimmer performs drownproof floating. This research team recommended treading in preference to drownproof floating in water temperature up to 68 degrees Fahrenheit.

Results of another study showed that approximately three times as much energy was required to accomplish the treading with head above the surface than was required by drownproof floating. Several years ago the writer observed that nonbuoyant students were unable to keep their heads above water while treading longer than fifteen minutes. Yet these same students, who could not float without motion, were able to sustain themselves at the surface for one hour, breathing every five or six seconds, while they performed a gentle travel stroke.

Most of the average floaters who tried to tread for one hour started to submerge repeatedly after thirty minutes. All of the average floaters found no difficulty whatsoever when asked to drownproof float for one hour. Nearly all good floaters (highly buoyant) were able to tread for one hour with their heads above the surface.

When asked to repeat these tests with the elimination of one or two arms, to simulate muscle cramps or injury to limbs, no student was able to tread with head above the surface longer than twenty minutes. All were able to perform drownproof floating for one hour, however, without the use of one arm, or without either.

The assumption that many people can tread water with

their heads above the surface for two hours must be seriously questioned. Experience has shown that only the highly buoyant, those who have received extensive aquatic training, or who are in excellent physical condition can endure even an hour of treading.

The fatigue which arises while people tread water with heads above the surface is a very significant factor. Estimated survival times in 60-degree water are over three hours for treading and over two hours for drownproof floating. Each of these survival times increases substantially as the 68-degree mark is approached. Based on energy cost of work, it is likely the drownproof floaters would last longer than the treaders in water between 60 and 68 degrees Fahrenheit.

Possibly the best course for anyone cast into cold water is to alternate treading with drownproof floating—the ratio of amount of treading or drownproof floating to depend on water temperature and fatigue. An appraisal of the use of a floating or swimming technique in cold water ought to take into consideration individual buoyancies, possibility of muscle cramps or injury to limbs, physical disabilities, energy cost of work, and body heat loss.

Sailors, Boaters, Canoeists, and Surfers

In many areas canoeists, boaters, and sailors are required to wear personal flotation devices while on the water. Many are told to hold on to the boat or canoe if cast overboard. But too often personal floation devices are not near at hand, or have not been worn, and boats drift away out of reach. This, then, leaves the boatsman, sailor, or canoeist in a precarious position, usually with clothes on, in a rough sea, a long distance from shore. How many people have tested themselves to be sure they could float long enough until help comes. How many, if shore were in sight, would be confident they could strike out for land and complete a mile or more of swimming?

Minimal requirements for swimming tests given to those who wish to sail, or paddle a canoe ought to be a mile swim and an hour float while fully clad. People who can swim only a distance of 100 or 200 yards may invite disaster when they decide to go canoeing or sailing, particularly if they fail to wear their personal flotation devices.

In Hawaii the writer was surprised to learn of the number of surfers who were either nonswimmers or weak swimmers. Although some tie themselves to their surfboards with a leash, they place themselves in great jeopardy whenever they fall into a high surf. When convinced they could learn to swim, these same surfers found that use of drownproofing techniques made things easy for them. They were able to float in high surf, swim to shore or to their surfboards while expending little energy. One surfer was so intrigued with drownproofing he completed a mile swim with wrists tied behind his back and feet tied together. He proved to himself he could swim a long distance with only a slight undulation of the body or the equivalent of the use of one limb.

Handicapped Persons

On one occasion, while visiting a Veteran's Hospital, the writer noticed an attendant taking a legless war veteran to the pool in a wheelchair. The wheelchair was directed down a ramp into the water. The veteran sat enjoying the water for a few minutes, and then was returned to the deck. When it became obvious the veteran could not swim, I asked him if he would like to learn. The request was greeted with zestful enthusiasm. After four hours of instruction in drownproof floating and the travel stroke this veteran was able to swim one half mile and float for thirty minutes.

One month later when I returned to the hospital to see how things were coming along, an attendant described the war veteran's daily practice: "We bring him to the pool at ten o'clock and he stays until noon. We bring him back at three and he won't leave until five." The veteran, an older man, grew to love swimming, and swam miles every day for the rest of his life.

Not only legless people, but those who have limited motion with arms, or those who have only two limbs available for use, can learn a variation of the travel stroke or drownproof floating.

Many tests which simulate cramps or injury to limbs have been administered to swimmers. Wrists were tied behind backs or legs tied in Buddha style. Swimmers were then asked to float long periods, swim long distances, perform certain water stunts including a forward and backward somersault, submerge themselves to a depth of twelve feet, swim underwater forty feet, and do all these tests in a continuous, non-stop fashion. Over ninety percent of the people who had previously learned the travel stroke and drownproof floating were able to accomplish these tests with flying colors. However, only thirty percent of those who had not learned drownproofing techniques were able to complete the tests. The energy conserving feature of drownproofing techniques makes it possible for those with disabled limbs to be able to swim and float for extended periods even when placed in stressful situations.

Whenever emotionally disturbed children have been taught drownproofing techniques, their instructors have been amazed at the calming effect of the floating and travel stroke. Apparently, participation in certain sports tends to excite these children, while the drownproofing maneuvers were an experience that provided a quiet, relaxed mode of activity.

OTHER FORMS OF SWIMMING

To the nonswimmer, drownproofing provides an excellent way of learning to float and swim. Nonswimmers and swimmers who learn drownproofing techniques are able to stay alive in the water for long periods. The principles of drownproofing are also applicable to the acquisition of the crawl, breast, and side strokes. The movement of the arms and legs, when performing *any* swimming stroke, becomes relatively easy for anyone who previously has learned to get a proper exchange of air while allowing body buoyancy to conserve energy.

Skin and scuba divers use drownproof floating techniques as they hover at the surface; they can don, remove, or adjust their equipment with little effort. Movement through the water with minimal expenditure of energy is fundamental to skin and scuba diving and makes it possible for thousands to extend their enjoyment of the water.

The skills of synchronized swimming require utmost control of breath and body position. Many adaptations of strokes are used as swimmers create their own variations. Mastery of drownproofing techniques are prerequisite to underwater body control and quick exchange of air. The various water stunts associated with synchronized swimming require smoothness and economy of effort with no gasping for air or spouting water at the surface. The grace of body movement through and under the water has led to the recognition of this popular sport by both participants and spectators.

Many people restrict their swimming at a lake or beach to wading in shallow water or lying in the sand—others are able to enjoy deep water without fear or frustration. People who are safe in the water can become involved in the limitless variety of aquatic activities.

Selected References

ADAMS, ROBERT. "Swimmers Are Taught Drownproofing." *The Haverhill Gazette*, Haverhill, Massachusetts, September 7, 1977.

BALTOZER, DIANE. "Drownproof: Learning to Save Yourself in Water." *The Quincy Patriot Ledger*, Quincy, Massachusetts, October 22, 1977.

BARTHELS, KATHERINE M. "Swimming Biomechanics: Resistance and Propulsion." *Swimming Technique*, Fall, 1977.

BENNET, JOSEPH. "A Stroke You Can Live With." *The Pittsburgh Press Roto*, Pittsburgh, Pennsylvania, January 29, 1978.

CASSIL, KAY. "Drownproofing: It Could Save Your Life." *McCall's*, May, 1978.

———. "This Could Save Your Life." *The Rhode Islander*, *Providence Journal Sunday Magazine*, Providence, Rhode Island, July 9, 1978.

———. "They Call It Drownproofing." *Wonderland: Grand Rapids Press Sunday Magazine*, Grand Rapids, Michigan, August 27, 1978.

———. "Swimming Coach Shows Potential Drowners How to Survive." *People*, June 18, 1979.

"Cold Water Survival—A Brief Presentation on Cold Water Safety." Canadian Red Cross Society With the Assistance of Mustang Sportswear Ltd., Vancouver, British Columbia, 1976.

COLLINS, DENNIS and KAY CASSIL. "Why Won't They Teach This Way to Stay Alive." *IPC Magazine*, London, England, 1979.

COUNCILMAN, JAMES E. "The Application of Bernouilli's Principle To Human Propulsion In Water." *Proceedings First International Symposium On Biomechanics In Swimming, Water Polo, and Diving*, September, 1970.

"Drownproofing Clinic Set at Talmadge Y.W.C.A." *Akron Beacon Journal*, Akron, Ohio, September 1, 1977.

"Drownproofing Course Saves Swimmers' Lives." *The American School Board Journal Insiders Report*, June 13, 1978.

"Drownproofing Courses." *The Chronicle of Higher Education*, March 13, 1978.

"Drownproof Swim Study on B. U. Slate." *Boston Globe*, Boston, Massachusetts, October 1, 1972.

D'ANTONIO, DENNIS. "Drownproofing Could Save 95% of All Victims." *National Enquirer*, August 23, 1977.

ENGEL, MURRY. "Teachers Instructed In Drownproofing." *Honolulu Star Bulletin*, Honolulu, Hawaii, June 18, 1979.

GOLDBERG, SHEP. "A Matter of Life and Death: Drownproofing." *Boston University News Release*, Boston University, Boston, Massachusetts, August 30, 1972.

GOLDEN, F. ST. C. "Cold Water Immersion." *Journal of Royal Naval Medical Service*, Winter, 1972.

_____. "Accidental Hypothermia." *Journal of Royal Naval Medical Service*, Winter, 1972.

GRAHAM, ROBERT. "The Comparative Energy Expenditure of Drownproofing and Treading Water." Unpublished

Master's Thesis, The University of Western Ontario, London, Ontario, August, 1974.

HAYWARD, JOHN S., ECKERSON, JOHN D., and COLLIS, MARTIN L. "Effect of Behavioral Variables On Cooling Rate Of Man In Cold Water." University of Victoria, Victoria, British Columbia, 1975.

KEATINGE, W. R. *Survival In Cold Water.* Oxford and Edinburgh; Blackwell Scientific Publications. 1969.

LANOUE, FRED. *Drownproofing a New Technique for Water Safety.* Engelwood Cliffs, New Jersey: Prentice-Hall, 1963.

ROY, HARCOURT. *Beginner's Guide to Swimming and Water Safety.* New York: Drake Publishers Inc., 1972.

SCOFIELD, JOHN. "Students Pass Test Tied Hand and Foot." part of "Character Marks the Coast Of Maine." *National Geographic*, Washington, D.C., June, 1968.

SHERBIN, JANET. "Drownproofing: You Need Not Drown." *Spectrum*, Boston University, Boston, Massachusetts, March 17, 1977.

SILVIA, CHARLES. *Manual and Lesson Plans for Basic Swimming, Water Stunts, Lifesaving, Springboard Diving, Skin and Scuba Diving. Methods of Teaching.* Springfield, Massachusetts. Privately published by the author, March, 1970.

SMITH, MURRAY. "A Theory Based Approach to Teaching Swimming," *Swimming II. Symposium On Biomechanics In Swimming.* Baltimore: University Park Press, 1975.

SOLOMON, NEIL. "Drownproofing Technique." *Boston Globe*, Boston, Massachusetts, June 23, 1977.

SURFACE, WILLIAM. "The Experts Differ on Water Safety." *Parade*, April 30, 1978.

Selected References   *165*

UNDERHILL, HAROLD. "Peace Corpsmen in Training Here: Curriculum Includes Ropes Course, Rock Climbing, Expeditions and Drownproofing." *The Island Times*, San Juan, Puerto Rico, September 8, 1961.

WEBB, DONALD. "Wetmore Instructs on Drownproofing." *Tuscaloosa News*, Tuscaloosa, Alabama, October 14, 1979.

WETMORE, REAGH. "Survival Swimming Techniques." *Journal of Physical Education and Recreation*, October, 1979.

_____. "Drownproof Swimming." *Life And Health*. Washington, D.C., June 1975.

_____. "Drownproof Swimming." *Good Health*, Warburton, Australia, November, 1975.

_____. "Fit for Aquatic Survival." *Aquatic World*. July, 1973.

_____. "Teaching Aquatic Survival." *Journal of Health, Physical Education and Recreation*, November/December, 1972.

_____. "A Technique of Self-Preservation: Drownproofing." *One Design and Off Shore Yachtsmen*, January, 1967.

_____. "How to Keep Alive Until Help Comes." *Popular Science*, July, 1967.

_____. *Instructors Manual for Drownproofing.* Groton, Massachusetts: Groton School Press, July, 1967.

_____. "Drownproofing." *Acadia Alumni Bulletin*, Acadia University, Wolfville, Nova Scotia, July, 1967.

_____. "Drownproofing." *The Independent School Bulletin*, National Association of Independent Schools. Boston, Massachusetts, October, 1965.

_____. "Drownproofing." *Andover Alumni Bulletin*, Phillips Academy, Andover, Massachusetts, April, 1965.

——. "Testing the Effectiveness of Individual Incentives Through Ropes Course, Track, and Drownproofing." *Journal of Health, Physical Education, and Recreation,* April, 1961.

——. "A Physical Education Program: Ropes Course, Track, and Drownproofing." American Academy of General Practice, Massachusetts Chapter, May, 1959.

WHITING, H. T. A. *Teaching The Persistent Nonswimmer.* New York: St. Martins Press, 1970.

WHITTEMORE, L. H. "Drownproofing: How to Stay Out of Trouble in the Water." *Parade*, New York, N.Y., July 17, 1977.

YUKIHIRO, DIANE. "Drownproofing: Water Safety Insurance." *Honolulu Advertiser,* Honolulu, Hawaii, June 19, 1979.

D R O W N P R O O F I N G : A Priority for Everyone

A 30-minute color/sound instructor training film.

Vision Associates
665 FIFTH AVENUE
NEW YORK, NEW YORK

Index

About the Author

Reagh C. Wetmore is the Director of Aquatics and Head Swimming Coach at Boston University. He believes drownproofing techniques should be "a priority for everyone." Over the past twenty-five years Dr. Wetmore has authored several articles on drownproofing, directed drownproofing programs for the Peace Corps and Outward Bound schools, and introduced drownproofing to a number of schools and universities throughout the country. He has conducted clinics at community centers, clubs, and colleges in the United States, Canada, and South America.

Dr. Wetmore has presented his drownproofing program on several television and radio shows, including NBC's "Today Show" and ABC's "Good Morning America." *Parade, McCall's, People* and other nationally syndicated newspapers and magazines have featured his adaptation of drownproofing techniques. He was the supervisor for the instructor training film, *Drownproofing: A Priority for Everyone* produced by Vision Associates of New York.

In the summer of 1979 Dr. Wetmore conducted a 6-day teacher/training institute on drownproofing for aquatic personnel in Hawaii. This clinic was sponsored by the Marine Advisory Program at the University of Hawaii and the State Department of Education of Hawaii to promote the inclusion of drownproofing in the public school curriculum.